Taking Care
of Myself

© Aladdin Books Ltd 2007

Designed and produced by
Aladdin Books Ltd
2/3 Fitzroy Mews
London W1T 6DF

First published in 2007
by Franklin Watts
338 Euston Road
London NW1 3BH

Franklin Watts Australia
Level 17/207 Kent Street
Sydney NSW 2000

Franklin Watts is a division of Hachette Children's Books.

ISBN 978 0 7496 7493 9

A catalogue record for
this book is available
from the British Library.

Illustrator: Christopher O'Neill

The author, Sarah Levete, has written and edited many books for young people
on social issues and other topics.

Dewey Classification:
363.1

Printed in China

THOUGHTS AND FEELINGS

Taking Care of Myself

Sarah Levete

Aladdin / Watts
London • Sydney

Contents

Happy And Healthy 6

Having Fun 11

Out And About 14

What Feels OK? 18

Standing Tall 23

Don't Forget 28

Find Out More 30

Index 32

Introduction

Read what the children in this book have to say about the different ways that they look after themselves. From a magic recipe for a healthy body to tips on dealing with bullies, they will give you hints on ways to keep happy and safe.

Happy And Healthy

Matt is congratulating Nick after their team won the football match at school. Matt knows all that exercise has made him a bit smelly, so he's going to shower first. A clean body is a happy and healthy body. Can you think of any other ways you can look after your body?

Your feet need a wash, too!

Can I shower first, Nick?

Yeah, I think you need to!

▶ Teeth Forever

Teeth are fussy. They need brushing twice a day after breakfast and before bed. For a dazzling smile, keep sweets and sugary drinks for special treats.

◀ Clean Hands

Germs are tiny living things which can give you coughs or tummy aches. The good news is they don't like soap and water! Wash and dry your hands before each meal and after you have played outside or been to the toilet. This will help keep germs down the plug-hole, where they belong!

▶ What A Pong!

After a day playing, a shower or bath helps to wash away dirt. It gets rid of nasty pongs, to make sure you smell nice! Remember your hair, too. It needs a brush twice a day. If your head feels itchy, tell your mum, dad or carer who will help you to get rid of any itchiness.

 Sweet Dreams

Your body works day and night to keep you healthy. After a busy day, it needs peace and quiet to give you energy for the next day. So, shut your eyes and dream… Goal!

Fun And Fit

Did you know that it is good for you to play outside? Exercise keeps you fit, so get moving! But always remember to tell an adult where you are.

Story: Paul's Sweet Tooth

1 Paul spent all his pocket money on sweets. He did not want to share them.

2 Paul ate the whole bag of sweets. He dropped the wrappers on the ground.

3 Paul's teeth kept the dentist very busy!

Why did Paul have to see the dentist?

He ate too many sweets. Sweets taste nice but they are not very kind to teeth. Try and eat them for treats only – they will taste even nicer! Always remember to put your litter in the bin. For a healthy body, from the top of your head to the tips of your toes, eat potatoes, rice, bread, or pasta with meat, fish, cheese or beans. And lots of fruit and vegetables. Delicious!

Here is Nick's magic recipe for a happy and healthy body!
"At meal times, eat up the foods which give you lots of energy.
But remember to wash and dry your hands before tucking in!"
Can you think of any other ways to keep happy and healthy?
What about a good night's sleep?"

Having Fun

Last week, Aaron was showing off. He climbed to the top of a tree. But he fell off and cut his knee – it really hurt. Phoebe was not impressed. She knows that play is only fun if it is safe. How do you have fun and keep safe?

▶ Tips For Fun Without Tears!

Learn your highway code.
And remember to use it all the
time, even when you're rushing
for an ice-cream!

◀ Keeping Safe

Keep away from railway lines or
building sites – they can be very
dangerous. When it's dark, play
inside. It's safer, and you can see
what you're doing! Tidy away
toys or you may trip over them.

▶ Water Safety

A dip in the pool or the
sea is great fun. But
you should always be
careful near water.
Make sure there is an
adult to watch you.
Don't push or jump on
other people and don't
get out of your depth.
Wear shoes if the
bottom is rocky – and
watch out for big waves!

Phoebe, what do you think about safety rules?

"All the 'do's and don'ts' can get boring. But remember that they keep you safe so you can have fun. A rule is easier to follow if it makes sense. So, if you don't understand a rule, ask."

Out And About

Charlotte and Lauren are going to buy a birthday present for Matt. Lauren says they need to make sure they have enough money for the phone, just in case of an emergency. Do you know how to stay safe when you are out and about? Read on and find out a few tips.

Always remember your phone number.

Have we got enough to buy a magazine as well?

Let's keep some change for the phone, in case we get lost.

Story: Jo Gets Lost

1 Jo was out with her dad and sister.

2 Jo's dad did not see Jo go into the shop. Soon she was lost.

3 A kind looking lady offered to help. Jo did not know her. What should she do?

What do you do if you get lost?

Don't panic! Even though it can be scary, there are several things you can do. Stay where you are, so that your carer or parent can come back and find you. If you can't see a police officer, go into a shop and ask the assistant to help. If a stranger offers to help, ask him or her to find a police officer. But don't go off with the stranger on your own.

Story: The Stranger

1 Tim was in the shop, buying sweets with his pocket money.

You haven't got enough for all of those.

Let me buy them for you. It's OK. I know your mum.

2 A man offered to buy them for him. Tim did not know the man.

I suppose it's OK if he knows Mum.

3 But Tim had been told not to accept things from strangers.

Should Tim accept the sweets from the man?

No. The man says he knows Tim's mum, but Tim is not sure. He doesn't know the man. When he gets home, Tim should tell his mum what the man said. Tim's mum will then tell him if he is allowed to accept the sweets from the man. Only accept something from a stranger, or from someone you do not know very well, if your mum, dad or carer has said that it is OK to do so.

▶ **Be Street Smart**

Most strangers would never do anything to hurt children. But some people are not so kind. It's hard to tell who is OK and who's not, so it's best not to talk to any strangers.

NO!!!

◀ **Need A Lift?**

Never accept a lift from a stranger or from someone you don't know well. Don't be afraid to say "NO!" If a stranger approaches you and asks you for help, walk the other way. Strangers should ask adults for help, not children.

Lauren, what are your safety tips?

"Never go off with a stranger. If you feel in danger, shout and run to a safe place. It's also safer to do things with friends – and more fun. Avoid places where no one is around, like woods or dark streets."

What Feels OK?

Last week, Cameron and Daisy's class talked about what feels OK and what doesn't feel OK. Daisy said surprises are OK, even though she finds it hard to keep secrets – she nearly told Nick about his birthday present! Cameron said that you should always tell someone if something doesn't feel OK. Do hugs make you feel OK?

A goodnight hug for sweet dreams.

Cameron, shall I tell you a secret?

But if you tell me, it won't be a secret!

What Feels Ok?

▶ Bad Touches

There are some touches which make you feel cosy. But there are others which may make you feel uncomfortable. If that is the case, always tell your mum, dad or another grown-up.

I don't like the way he touches me.

Come and sit with me.

Don't do that. It really hurts.

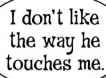

◀ Hey, That Hurts!

If you are playing and someone hurts you, tell the person to stop. If he or she doesn't stop, tell a grown-up. Nobody should hurt you, by accident or on purpose. If it happens, tell someone.

▶ Good Touches

A good touch makes you feel nice and safe. If you are told to keep a touch a secret, or if you don't like the touch, tell another grown-up. A good touch should never, ever be a secret.

Can you keep a secret? There's a surprise party for Ashya.

Story: Keeping a Secret

1 Kay's friends told her about a surprise party.

If you tell your mum I hurt you, she will be very cross with you.

2 Later that day, Kay's babysitter told Kay to keep a secret about being hurt.

A secret about a party is nice. But being hit should not be a secret.

3 Kay was confused. The babysitter's secret made her feel uncomfortable.

Should Kay keep both secrets?

No. Good secrets about a surprise, like Ashya's party, should be kept. But secrets which can upset or hurt you, or someone else, should not be kept. If a secret makes you uncomfortable, tell an adult you trust – perhaps your mum, dad or a teacher. Can you think of examples of secrets to keep and secrets to tell?

▶ To Tell Or Not To Tell?

Even if you have been told how important it is to keep a secret, if it doesn't make you feel OK, tell a grown-up you trust.

▼ Being Nice

Nobody should do or say things which may hurt someone else. For instance, saying nasty things about a person can be very upsetting. So if someone you know is feeling sad, why not be extra kind to them?

Cameron, can you keep a secret?

"No problem. But only if it's a nice secret. If a secret makes me or someone else unhappy, then I will tell a grown-up. And if, for some reason, he or she doesn't believe me, I will go on and on telling it, until someone does believe me."

Standing Tall

Bullying is always wrong. Scott was bullied at school and it made him very unhappy until he told a teacher who made sure the bullying stopped.

What do you do if you are being bullied, or if you know that someone else is being bullied?

No one should ever be bullied.

Bullying makes people very unhappy.

▶ Hitting Back

Some people think that hitting back at bullies is the way to deal with them. But it doesn't work and it certainly doesn't make the problem go away. It can even get you into trouble. The best way of dealing with the problem of bullies is to tell an adult you trust.

◀ Say "No". Tell Someone.

If you are being bullied, or know that it is happening to someone else, there are several things you can do. You can say "NO!" to the bully. If that doesn't work, tell a grown-up who will know how to help you. Don't be scared of telling. It is the bravest thing to do.

Story: Tom Picks on Ann

1 Tom was choosing people for his game.

Ugh. We don't want her. She's no good.

2 After what Tom said, Ann felt lonely and sad.

He's always so nasty to me.

Take no notice of Tom. He thinks he's being clever, but he's just being mean.

3 Raj didn't like the way Tom picked on Ann. He decided to stick up for Ann.

Is Tom bullying Ann?

Bullying isn't just about hurting someone physically. Making nasty comments about someone and leaving someone out on purpose is bullying. Making threats against someone or damaging his or her belongings is bullying. Raj knows that all bullying is wrong. He wants to help Ann.

I can just ignore them.

▶ No More Bullying!

Stop bullying by telling someone about it.
Some people can ignore nasty comments
and stand tall. If ignoring a bully
doesn't work, tell a grown-up. In the
end, telling will also help the bully.
Bullies are often unhappy and
need help.

I'm glad
I told you,
Mr Khan.

▼ Bored Of Being A Bully...

Bullies love to get a reaction. They
think it's fun. If you keep calm and
hide your feelings, they might get
bored and leave you alone. It makes
it harder for them to bully you if it
seems like you don't care.

I'm fed up
being horrible.

Scott, what can be done about bullying?
"Don't give up. Bullying is wrong so it is always right to tell.
Telling your mum, dad, carer or teacher will put a stop to bullying.
It's important to tell if you know that someone else is being bullied."

Don't Forget...

1

What do you think is the most important thing about looking after yourself, Cameron?

"The thing that matters most to me is telling the person who is looking after me how I feel. If I don't feel well, it's important someone knows. It's no good keeping it a secret, is it? It always makes me feel better if I talk to Mum or Dad about it."

2

How do you keep safe and happy, Lauren?

"I know that it is very important to say 'NO!' if something doesn't feel right. It doesn't mean being rude. It just means being firm. At school, we practised saying 'NO!' to each other. It was quite difficult, so I practised at home in front of a mirror! And I know how to make an emergency telephone call."

What's your tip for feeling good, Phoebe?

"Some days I get grumpy if I've been told off. But being grumpy doesn't make me feel good, so I say sorry as soon as possible. Then I can stop feeling grumpy and can enjoy the rest of my day!

If I feel cross with someone, I try to talk calmly to the person about how I feel. Then we can be friends again!"

3

4

How do you stay healthy and happy, Nick?

"I keep fit and well by eating lots of healthy foods. I really like playing football in the park. It's good fun and it's healthy too!

But after a game, I need a good wash! When I'm playing, I know that it's important to think about what is safe. I always make sure that mum or dad, or the person who is looking after me, knows where I am."

Find Out More About Keeping Safe

Helpful Addresses and Phone Numbers

Talking about problems can really help. If you can't talk to someone close to you, then try ringing one of these organisations:

Childline
Tel: 0800 1111
A 24-hour free helpline for children. The number won't show up on a telephone bill.

Kidscape
2 Grosvenor Gardens,
London SW1W 0DP
Tel: 020 7730 3300 (Mon-Fri 10am-4pm). A helpline for parents of bullied or bullying children. Send a large SAE for copies of their booklets.

NSPCC (National Society for the Prevention of Cruelty to Children)
Tel: 0800 800 500
A 24-hour free helpline for anyone worried about child safety.

Kids Helpline, Australia
Tel: 1800 55 1800
A 24-hour free helpline for children. Kids Helpline also offers online counselling either via the web or email at www.kidshelp.com.au

Kidsafe, Australia
Tel: 02 6290 2244 (ACT branch)
This organisation helps to prevent injuries to children. It has individual branches in every state.

On the Web

These websites are also helpful. You can get in touch with some of them using email:

www.childline.org.uk

www.suzylamplugh.org/smartkids

www.kidsmart.org.uk

www.hedgehogs.gov.uk

www.kidsafe.com.au

www.kidshelp.com.au

www.childnet-int.org

www.kidpower.org

Further Reading

If you want to read more about personal safety, try:

Talking About: Keeping Safe by Sarah Levete (Aladdin/Watts)

Choices and Decisions: Dealing with Bullying by Pete Sanders (Franklin Watts)

Talking About: Eating and Health by Sarah Levete (Aladdin/Watts)

Safety Kids Club: Kids Keeping Kids Safe by K L Wheatley (Leading Edge Publishing)

Keeping Healthy by Jo Ellen Moor (Evan-Moor Educational Publishers)

The Safe Zone: A Kid's Guide to Personal Safety by Donna Chaiet and Francine Russell (HarperCollins)

Index

Accepting lifts or presents
  16, 17

Bullying 23-27

Cleaning your teeth 7

Emergencies 14, 28
Exercise 8

Feeling
  OK 17, 18, 19, 20
  unhappy or sad 21, 23, 25

Getting lost 15
Good and bad touches 19

Healthy body 6, 8, 9, 10
Healthy eating 9, 10, 29

Highway code 12
Hugs 18, 19

Playing safely 11, 12, 13, 29

Rules, rules, rules 13

Saying "NO!" 5, 17, 24, 28
Secrets 18, 20, 22, 28
Sleeping well 8, 10
Strangers 15, 16, 17
Sweet tooth 9

Telephone calls 14, 28
Telling a grown-up 17, 19,
  20, 21, 22, 24, 26, 27, 28

Washing 6, 7, 10, 29
Water safety 12

Photocredits

l-left, r-right, b-bottom, t-top, c-centre, m-middle

All photos from istockphoto.com except: Cover tl — Digital Vision.

Cover tc, 12 — TongRo Image Stock. 26 — DAJ.

All the photos in this book have been posed by models.